pies

pies

delicious homemade pie recipes

This edition published in 2010
LOVE FOOD is an imprint of Parragon Books Ltd

Parragon
Queen Street House
4 Queen Street
Bath BA1 1HE, UK

ISBN: 978-1-4454-0700-5

Printed in China

Produced by the Bridgewater Book Company Ltd
Design concept by Fiona Roberts
Photographer: Laurie Evans
Home economist: Annie Rigg

Notes for the Reader
This book uses imperial, metric, and US cup measurements. Follow the same units of
measurement throughout; do not mix imperial and metric. All spoon measurements are
level: teaspoons are assumed to be 5 ml, and tablespoons are assumed to be 15 ml. Unless
otherwise stated, milk is assumed to be whole, eggs and individual vegetables such as
potatoes are medium, and pepper is freshly ground black pepper.

The times given are an approximate guide only. Preparation times differ according to the
techniques used by different people and the cooking times may also vary from those given
as a result of the type of oven used. Optional ingredients, variations or serving suggestions
have not been included in the calculations.

Recipes using raw or very lightly cooked eggs should be avoided by infants, the elderly,
pregnant women, convalescents, and anyone with a chronic condition. Pregnant and
breastfeeding women are advised to avoid eating peanuts and peanut products. Sufferers
from nut allergies should be aware that some of the ready-prepared ingredients used in the
recipes in this book may contain nuts. Always check the packaging before use.

contents

Introduction

Homemade pies are "proper" cooking, like our moms and grandmothers used to do, and they are just as satisfying to make today. They will also be greeted with the same relish and delight by another generation of family and friends.

Clear, step-by-step instructions ensure that you don't have to be a culinary genius to make melt-in-the-mouth pie dough. In fact, for many of the recipes in this book, you don't have to make pie dough at all. Many traditional favorites, such as Key Lime Pie, are made with a cookie crumb crust, while Chocolate Chiffon Pie uses ground Brazil nuts. All you need is a food processor to whiz up the ingredients in moments.

However, sweet pies made with pie dough—whether single or double crust—are among everybody's top ten choices for desserts and snacks with tea or coffee. We all deserve a treat from time to time, in the form of a generous helping of pie.

The secret to successful dough is to handle it as little as possible and to keep it cool. Don't skip the instruction to chill it in the refrigerator before rolling out, as this process ensures that it will be light and crisp when cooked. Do make sure that the oven is preheated, and if the shell is baked blind (that is, without filling), line the shell with parchment paper and fill it with dried beans, purpose-made ceramic beans, metal beans, or rice, to stop the base from bubbling up and cooking unevenly while it is baking.

This is a chapter full of family favorites and comfort foods that take us back to the days of our childhood. The delicious aroma of apples and spices as they bake in the oven, the sheer sticky pleasure of plunging a spoon into a gooey chocolate filling, and the melt-in-the-mouth contrast of sharp citrus and sweet meringue transport us back to days that seem to have been less troublesome, much sunnier, and, unquestionably, sweeter.

There is no doubt why these recipes have become classics, and the great thing is that they are so easy to recreate yet the results are quite magical. Even the most inexperienced cook will have no trouble rustling up that great delight, Banoffee Pie, for example, and it is absolutely guaranteed to enchant kids of all ages.

CLASSIC PIES

There are double-crust and single-crust pies, some of them best served piping hot straight from the oven, others at their most delicious if eaten while still warm, and some where gratification must be deferred until they have cooled completely or even chilled for a while. In other words, there is something for everyone. Some are so rich that no one, however sweet-toothed, can manage more than a small slice at any one time, while others are sure to inspire requests for a second helping. The delicious fillings include fruit, chocolate, nuts, and corn syrup which contrast and mingle mouthwateringly with crisp pie dough or crunchy cookie-crumb crusts.

SERVES 6

PIE DOUGH

generous 2⅜ cups all-purpose flour

pinch of salt

3 oz/85 g butter or margarine, cut
    into small pieces

3 oz/85 g lard or vegetable
    shortening, cut into small pieces

about 6 tbsp cold water

beaten egg or milk, for glazing

FILLING

1 lb 10 oz–2 lb 4 oz/750 g–1 kg
    cooking apples, peeled, cored,
    and sliced

scant ⅔ cup packed brown or
    superfine sugar, plus extra
    for sprinkling

½–1 tsp ground cinnamon, allspice,
    or ground ginger

1–2 tbsp water (optional)

Traditional Apple Pie

This apple pie has a double
crust and is delicious either
hot or cold. The apples
can be flavored with other
spices or grated citrus rind.

- To make the pie dough, sift the flour and salt into a large bowl. Add the butter and fat and rub in with the fingertips until the mixture resembles fine bread crumbs. Add the water and gather the mixture together into a dough. Wrap the dough and let chill in the refrigerator for 30 minutes.
- Preheat the oven to 425°F/220°C. Roll out almost two-thirds of the pie dough thinly and use to line a deep 9-inch/23-cm pie plate or pie pan.
- Mix the apples with the sugar and spice and pack into the pastry shell; the filling can come up above the rim. Add the water if needed, particularly if the apples are a dry variety.
- Roll out the remaining pie dough to form a lid. Dampen the edges of the pie rim with water and position the lid, pressing the edges firmly together. Trim and crimp the edges.
- Use the trimmings to cut out leaves or other shapes to decorate the top of the pie, dampen and attach. Glaze the top of the pie with beaten egg or milk, make 1–2 slits in the top, and place the pie on a baking sheet.
- Bake in the preheated oven for 20 minutes, then reduce the temperature to 350°F/180°C and bake for a further 30 minutes, or until the pastry is a light golden brown. Serve hot or cold, sprinkled with sugar.

SERVES 4
FILLING
generous 3⅜ cups canned
    sweetened condensed milk
4 ripe bananas
juice of ½ lemon
1 tsp vanilla extract
2 cups heavy cream, whipped
2¾ oz/75 g semisweet chocolate,
    grated

COOKIE CRUST
3 oz/85 g butter, melted, plus
    extra for greasing
5½ oz/150 g graham crackers,
    crushed into crumbs
scant ⅓ cup shelled almonds,
    toasted and ground
scant ⅓ cup shelled hazelnuts,
    toasted and ground

Banoffee Pie

A melt-in-the-mouth combination of rich toffee and ripe bananas, topped with grated semisweet chocolate, this American pie has become a firm family favorite throughout the world.

• Place the unopened cans of milk in a large pan and add enough water to cover them. Bring to a boil, then reduce the heat and let simmer for 2 hours, topping up the water level to keep the cans covered. Carefully lift out the hot cans from the pan and let cool.

• Preheat the oven to 350°F/180°C. Grease a 9-inch/23-cm tart pan with butter. Place the remaining butter in a bowl and add the crushed graham crackers and ground nuts. Mix together well, then press the mixture evenly into the base and side of the tart pan. Bake for 10–12 minutes, then remove from the oven and let cool.

• Peel and slice the bananas and place in a bowl. Squeeze over the juice from the lemon, add the vanilla extract, and mix together. Spread the banana mixture over the cookie crust in the pan, then spoon the contents of the cooled cans of condensed milk over the bananas. Sprinkle over 1¾ oz/50 g of the chocolate, then top with a layer of whipped cream. Sprinkle over the remaining grated chocolate and serve the pie at room temperature.

SERVES 4

PIE DOUGH

generous 1 cup all-purpose flour,
    plus extra for dusting
1¾ oz/50 g butter, cut into small
    pieces, plus extra for greasing

¼ cup confectioners' sugar, sifted
finely grated rind of ½ lemon
½ egg yolk, beaten
1½ tbsp milk
4 tbsp strawberry preserve

FILLING

3½ oz/100 g butter
½ cup packed brown sugar
2 eggs, beaten
1 tsp almond extract
¾ cup rice flour
3 tbsp ground almonds
3 tbsp slivered almonds, toasted
confectioners' sugar, to decorate

Bakewell Tart

This traditional English dessert was originally known as Bakewell pie. Strawberry preserve topped with a delicious almond mixture makes this tart very difficult to resist. It is best served warm.

• To make the pie dough, sift the flour into a bowl. Rub in the butter with the fingertips until the mixture resembles fine bread crumbs. Mix in the confectioners' sugar, lemon rind, egg yolk, and milk. Knead briefly on a lightly floured counter. Wrap the dough and let chill in the refrigerator for 30 minutes.

• Preheat the oven to 375°F/190°C. Grease an 8-inch/20-cm ovenproof tart pan. Roll out the pie dough to a thickness of ¼ inch/5 mm and use it to line the base and side of the pan. Prick all over the base with a fork, then spread with the preserve.

• To make the filling, cream the butter and sugar together until fluffy. Gradually beat in the eggs, followed by the almond extract, rice flour, and ground almonds. Spread the mixture evenly over the preserve-covered pie dough, then sprinkle over the slivered almonds. Bake in the oven for 40 minutes until golden. Remove from the oven, dust with confectioners' sugar, and serve warm.

SERVES 8

PIE DOUGH

scant 1⅝ cups all-purpose flour,
    plus extra for dusting

2 tbsp unsweetened cocoa

5 oz/140 g butter

2 tbsp superfine sugar

1–2 tbsp cold water

FILLING

6 oz/175 g butter

scant 1¾ cups packed brown sugar

4 eggs, lightly beaten

4 tbsp unsweetened cocoa, sifted

5½ oz/150 g semisweet chocolate

1¼ cups light cream

1 tsp chocolate extract

TO DECORATE

scant 2 cups heavy cream, whipped

chocolate flakes and curls

Mississippi Mud Pie

To melt chocolate, break it into small pieces and place in a heatproof bowl set over a pan of barely simmering water. Do not let the base of the bowl come into contact with the surface of the water.

• To make the pie dough, sift the flour and cocoa into a mixing bowl. Rub in the butter with the fingertips until the mixture resembles fine bread crumbs. Stir in the sugar and enough cold water to mix to a soft dough. Wrap the dough and let chill in the refrigerator for 15 minutes.

• Preheat the oven to 375°F/190°C. Roll out the dough on a lightly floured counter and use to line a 9-inch/23-cm loose-bottom tart pan or ceramic pie dish. Line with parchment paper and fill with dried beans. Bake in the oven for 15 minutes. Remove from the oven and take out the paper and beans. Bake the pastry shell for an additional 10 minutes.

• To make the filling, beat the butter and sugar together in a bowl and gradually beat in the eggs with the cocoa. Melt the chocolate (see Note, left) and beat it into the mixture with the light cream and the chocolate extract.

• Reduce the oven temperature to 325°F/160°C. Pour the mixture into the pastry shell and bake for 45 minutes, or until the filling has set gently.

• Let the mud pie cool completely, then transfer it to a serving plate, if you like. Cover with the whipped cream.

• Decorate the pie with chocolate flakes and curls and then let chill until ready to serve.

SERVES 8

2 tbsp butter, plus extra for greasing

2½ cups milk

generous 1 cup superfine sugar

finely grated rind of 1 orange

4 eggs, separated

1⅜ cups fresh white bread crumbs

pinch of salt

6 tbsp orange marmalade

Queen of Puddings

This is a slightly different version of an old favorite, made with the addition of orange rind and marmalade to give a deliciously zesty citrus flavor.

• Preheat the oven to 350°F/180°C. Grease a 6-cup ovenproof dish.

• To make the custard, heat the milk in a pan with the butter, ⅓ cup of the sugar and the grated orange rind until just warm.

• Whisk the egg yolks in a bowl. Gradually pour the warm milk over the eggs, stirring constantly.

• Stir the bread crumbs into the custard, then transfer the mixture to the prepared dish and let stand for about 15 minutes.

• Bake in the oven for 20–25 minutes, or until the custard has just set. Remove the dish from the oven, but do not turn off the oven.

• To make the meringue, whisk the egg whites with the salt in a clean, greasefree bowl until soft peaks form. Whisk in the remaining sugar, a little at a time.

• When cool, gently spread the orange marmalade over the cooked custard. It is not necessary for the meringue to be smooth—it usually looks better in little peaks. Use a palette knife for spreading, or pipe the meringue on top.

• Return the pudding to the oven and bake for an additional 20 minutes until the meringue is crisp and golden. Serve warm.

SERVES 8
PIE DOUGH
scant 1¼ cups all-purpose flour
2 tbsp superfine sugar
4 oz/115 g butter, cut into small
    pieces
1 tbsp water

FILLING
3 eggs
⅓ cup superfine sugar
⅔ cup light cream
⅔ cup milk
freshly grated nutmeg
whipped cream (optional), to serve

Custard Pie

This is a classic egg custard pie, which should be served as fresh as possible for the best flavor and texture. Baking the pastry shell blind ensures that the finished pie has a crisp base.

• To make the pie dough, place the flour and sugar in a mixing bowl. Rub in the butter with the fingertips until the mixture resembles fine bread crumbs. Add the water and mix together until a soft dough has formed. Wrap the dough and let chill in the refrigerator for 30 minutes.

• Roll out the dough to a circle slightly larger than a 9½-inch/24-cm loose-bottom tart pan.

• Line the pan with the dough, trimming off the edge. Prick all over the base with a fork and let chill in the refrigerator for about 30 minutes.

• Preheat the oven to 375°F/190°C. Line the pastry shell with parchment paper and fill with dried beans. Bake in the oven for 15 minutes. Remove the paper and beans and bake the pastry shell for an additional 15 minutes.

• To make the filling, whisk the eggs, sugar, cream, milk, and nutmeg together. Pour the filling into the prepared pastry shell.

• Return the pie to the oven and cook for an additional 25–30 minutes, or until the filling is just set. Serve with whipped cream, if you like.

SERVES 8
CRUMB CRUST
6 oz/175 g graham crackers
or ginger snaps
2 tbsp superfine sugar
½ tsp ground cinnamon
2½ oz/70 g butter, melted

FILLING
butter, for greasing
1¾ cups canned
sweetened condensed milk
½ cup freshly squeezed lime juice
finely grated rind of 3 limes
4 egg yolks
whipped cream, to serve

Key Lime Pie

This pie dates from the late 1850s, when canned condensed milk first became available—a welcome development in the remote Florida Keys, where fresh milk was a luxury. Key limes aren't commercially grown elsewhere and their season is short, so ordinary limes are most frequently used in this all-American favorite.

• Preheat the oven to 325°F/160°C. Lightly grease a 9-inch/23-cm pie plate, about 1½ inches/4 cm deep.
• To make the crumb crust, place the crackers, sugar, and cinnamon in a food processor and process until fine crumbs form—do not overprocess to a powder. Add the melted butter and process again until moistened.
• Tip the crumb mixture into the pie plate and press over the base and up the side. Place the pie plate on a baking sheet and bake in the oven for 5 minutes.
• Meanwhile, beat the condensed milk, lime juice, lime rind, and egg yolks together in a bowl until well blended.
• Remove the crumb crust from the oven, pour the filling into the crumb crust, and spread out to the edge. Return to the oven for an additional 15 minutes, or until the filling is set around the edge but still wobbly in the center.
• Let cool completely on a wire rack, then cover and let chill for at least 2 hours. Serve spread thickly with whipped cream.

SERVES 4

PIE DOUGH

generous 1 cup all-purpose flour,
  plus extra for dusting

3 oz/85 g butter, cut into small
  pieces, plus extra for greasing

¼ cup confectioners' sugar, sifted

finely grated rind of ½ lemon

½ egg yolk, beaten

1½ tbsp milk

FILLING

3 tbsp cornstarch

1¼ cups water

juice and grated rind of 2 lemons

generous ¾ cup superfine sugar

2 eggs, separated

Lemon Meringue Pie

A combination of tangy lemon and soft meringue, this is a classic dessert, which is ideal for both dinner parties and family meals.

• To make the pie dough, sift the flour into a bowl. Rub in the butter with the fingertips until the mixture resembles fine bread crumbs. Mix in the remaining ingredients. Knead briefly on a lightly floured counter. Let rest for 30 minutes.

• Preheat the oven to 350°F/180°C. Grease an 8-inch/20-cm pie dish with butter. Roll out the pie dough to a thickness of ¼ inch/5 mm; use it to line the base and sides of the dish. Prick all over with a fork, line with parchment paper and fill with dried beans. Bake for in the oven for 15 minutes. Remove from the oven and take out the paper and beans. Reduce the temperature to 300°F/150°C.

• To make the filling, mix the cornstarch with a little of the water. Place the remaining water in a pan. Stir in the lemon juice and rind and cornstarch paste. Bring to a boil, stirring. Cook for 2 minutes. Let cool a little. Stir in 5 tablespoons of the sugar and the egg yolks and pour into the pastry shell.

• Whisk the egg whites in a clean, greasefree bowl until stiff. Whisk in the remaining sugar and spread over the pie. Bake for another 40 minutes. Remove from the oven, cool, and serve.

Individual pies always seem special, whether they are served as a dessert or as a delightful snack to accompany a cup of tea or coffee—or even, Continental-style, a glass of wine. Children, in particular, love having their very own pie; it certainly makes serving easier, especially when you're feeding an odd number of people.

The delightful range of sweet treats on offer in this chapter are extra special because not only are they extremely attractive and tempting, but they are also absolutely scrumptious. Who could resist cute little Banana Pies or elegant Chocolate Blueberry Pies? There's even a recipe for delicious Paper-Thin Fruit Pies, designed for those who are watching their weight and intake of fats and sugars.

SWEET SNACKS

As well as these delightful little pies, the recipes in this chapter also include a fabulous collection of strudels, those melt-in-the-mouth, wafer-thin layered confections created by the master bakers of Vienna. Fortunately, you don't have to serve a long apprenticeship to learn the art of making strudel pastry, as nowadays the closely related phyllo pastry is widely available. Of course, you don't have to tell your guests that you "cheated"; just bask in their admiration of your amazing skills.

There are imaginative twists on a variety of other European specialties, as well as some lovely ideas from the New World, too. And, what's more, the simple-to-follow recipes prove that you don't have to be an expert to produce an array of truly tempting sweet delights that would make even a professional pâtissier proud.

MAKES 16

PIE DOUGH

1 lb/450 g all-purpose flour, plus
    extra for dusting

5 tbsp lard or vegetable shortening,
    cut into small pieces

5 tbsp butter, preferably unsalted,
    cut into small pieces

1–2 tbsp cold water

FILLING

2 large bananas

⅓ cup finely chopped no-soak
    dried apricots

pinch of grated nutmeg

dash of orange juice

1 egg yolk, beaten

confectioners' sugar, for dusting

cream or ice cream, to serve

Banana Pies

These miniature pies require a little time to prepare, but are well worth the effort and are sure to be popular. A sweet banana filling is wrapped in pie dough and baked until golden brown.

• To make the pie dough, sift the flour into a large bowl. Add the lard and butter and rub into the flour with the fingertips until the mixture resembles bread crumbs. Gradually blend in the water to make a soft dough. Wrap the dough and let chill in the refrigerator for 30 minutes.

• Preheat the oven to 350°F/180°C. Peel the bananas and mash in a bowl with a fork, then stir in the apricots, nutmeg, and orange juice, mixing well.

• Roll out the dough on a lightly floured counter and cut out 16 x 4-inch/10-cm circles.

• Spoon a little of the banana filling onto one half of each circle and fold the pastry over the filling to form semicircles. Pinch the sides together and seal by pressing the edges with a fork.

• Arrange the pies on a nonstick baking sheet and brush them lightly with the beaten egg yolk to glaze. Cut a small slit in each pie and cook in the preheated oven for 25 minutes, or until golden brown.

• Dust the banana pies with confectioners' sugar and serve with cream or ice cream.

MAKES 12

PIE DOUGH

1 cup all-purpose flour, plus extra for
   dusting

3 oz/85 g butter, cut into small pieces

generous ¼ cup golden superfine
   sugar

2 egg yolks

FILLING

2 tbsp maple syrup

⅔ cup heavy cream

scant ⅝ cup golden superfine sugar

pinch of cream of tartar

6 tbsp water

1 cup shelled pecans, chopped

12 pecan halves, to decorate

Maple Pecan Pies

Maple syrup and pecans give a wonderful flavor to the toffee filling in these little pies. Serve on their own, or with some whipped cream.

• To make the pie dough, sift the flour into a mixing bowl and rub in the butter with the fingertips until the mixture resembles bread crumbs. Add the sugar and egg yolks and mix to form a soft dough. Wrap the dough and let chill in the refrigerator for 30 minutes. Preheat the oven to 400°F/200°C.

• On a lightly floured counter, roll out the pie dough thinly, cut out 12 circles, and use to line 12 tartlet pans. Prick the bases with a fork. Line with parchment paper and fill with dried beans. Bake in the oven for 10–15 minutes, or until light golden. Remove from the oven and take out the paper and beans. Bake the pastry shells for an additional 2–3 minutes. Let cool on a wire rack.

• Mix half the maple syrup and half the cream in a bowl. Place the sugar, cream of tartar, and water in a pan and heat gently until the sugar dissolves. Bring to a boil and boil until light golden. Remove from the heat and stir in the maple syrup and cream mixture.

• Return the pan to the heat and cook to the soft ball stage (240°F/116°C): that is, when a little of the mixture dropped into a bowl of cold water forms a soft ball. Stir in the remaining cream and leave until cool. Brush the remaining maple syrup over the edges of the pies. Place the chopped pecans in the pastry shells and spoon in the toffee. Top each pie with a pecan half. Let cool completely before serving.

SERVES 6

5½ oz/150 g butter, preferably
    unsalted, plus extra for greasing
generous 1¼ cups mixed chopped
    nuts
4 oz/115 g semisweet chocolate,
    chopped

4 oz/115 g milk chocolate, chopped
4 oz/115 g white chocolate, chopped
7 oz/200 g phyllo pastry, thawed if
    frozen
3 tbsp corn syrup
½ cup confectioners' sugar
cream, to serve

Chocolate Nut Strudel

This is an indulgent chocolate version of a classic strudel. It is delicious served with cream.

• Preheat the oven to 375°F/190°C. Lightly grease a baking sheet with butter. Set aside 1 tablespoon of the nuts. Mix the 3 types of chocolate together.

• Place 1 sheet of phyllo on a clean dish towel. Melt the butter and brush the sheet of phyllo with the butter, drizzle with a little syrup, and sprinkle with some nuts and chocolate. Place another sheet of phyllo on top and repeat until you have used all the nuts and chocolate.

• Use the dish towel to help you carefully roll up the strudel and place on the baking sheet, drizzle with a little more syrup, and sprinkle with the reserved nuts. Bake in the preheated oven for 20–25 minutes. If the nuts start to brown too much, cover the strudel with a sheet of foil.

• Sprinkle the strudel with confectioners' sugar, slice, and eat warm with cream.

MAKES 4

1 eating apple

1 ripe pear

2 tbsp lemon juice

4 tbsp lowfat spread

4 sheets phyllo pastry, thawed
    if frozen

2 tbsp reduced-sugar apricot preserve

1 tbsp unsweetened orange juice

1 tbsp finely chopped pistachios

2 tsp confectioners' sugar, for dusting

Paper-Thin Fruit Pies

These extra-crisp phyllo pastry shells, filled with slices of fruit and glazed with apricot preserve, make a fabulous dessert for the sweet-toothed who are trying to follow a healthy diet.

• Preheat the oven to 400°F/200°C. Core and thinly slice the apple and pear and immediately toss them in the lemon juice to prevent them from turning brown. Melt the lowfat spread in a pan over low heat.

• Cut each sheet of pastry into 4 and cover with a clean, damp dish towel. Brush a 4-cup nonstick muffin pan (cup size 4 inches/10 cm in diameter) with a little of the lowfat spread.

• Working on each pie separately, brush 4 small sheets of pastry with lowfat spread. Press a sheet of pastry into the base of 1 cup. Arrange the other sheets of pastry on top at slightly different angles. Repeat with the other sheets of pastry to make another 3 pies.

• Arrange the apple and pear slices alternately in the center of each pie shell and lightly crimp the edge of the pastry of each pie.

• Stir the preserve and orange juice together until smooth and brush over the fruit. Bake in the preheated oven for 12–15 minutes. Sprinkle with the pistachios, dust lightly with confectioners' sugar, and serve hot straight from the oven.

SERVES 2–4

8 crisp eating apples

1 tbsp lemon juice

2/3 cup golden raisins

1 tsp ground cinnamon

1/2 tsp grated nutmeg

1 tbsp brown sugar

6 sheets phyllo pastry, thawed
   if frozen

vegetable oil spray

confectioners' sugar, to serve

SAUCE

1 tbsp cornstarch

2 cups hard cider

Apple Strudel and Cider Sauce

This light, crisp, and spicy strudel is delicious served either warm or cold. Here it is served with a hot cider sauce, but it also goes well with whipped cream or ice cream.

• Preheat the oven to 375°F/190°C. Line a baking sheet with parchment paper.

• Peel and core the apples and chop them into 1/2-inch/1-cm dice. Toss the apples in a bowl with the lemon juice, golden raisins, cinnamon, nutmeg, and brown sugar.

• Lay out a sheet of phyllo pastry, spray with vegetable oil, and lay a second sheet on top. Repeat with a third sheet. Spread over half the apple mixture and roll up lengthwise, tucking in the ends to enclose the filling. Repeat to make a second strudel. Slide onto the baking sheet, spray with oil, and bake for 15–20 minutes.

• To make the sauce, blend the cornstarch in a pan with a little hard cider until smooth. Add the remaining cider and heat gently, stirring, until the mixture boils and thickens. Serve the strudel warm or cold, dredged with confectioners' sugar, and accompanied by the cider sauce.

MAKES 10

PIE DOUGH

scant 1¼ cups all-purpose flour

½ cup unsweetened cocoa

generous ¼ cup superfine sugar

pinch of salt

4½ oz/125 g butter, cut into
    small pieces

1 egg yolk

1–2 tbsp cold water

SAUCE

1⅜ cups blueberries

2 tbsp crème de cassis

scant ⅛ cup confectioners' sugar,
    sifted

FILLING

5 oz/140 g semisweet chocolate

1 cup heavy cream

⅔ cup sour cream

Chocolate Blueberry Pies

The combination of chocolate pie dough, rich filling, and glistening berries makes these pies very impressive. They look pretty with a little confectioners' sugar sifted over them just before serving.

• To make the pie dough, place the flour, cocoa, sugar, and salt in a large bowl and rub in the butter until the mixture resembles bread crumbs. Add the egg and a little cold water to form a dough. Wrap the dough and let chill in the refrigerator for 30 minutes.

• Remove the pie dough from the refrigerator and roll out. Use to line 10 x 4-inch/10-cm tart pans. Freeze for 30 minutes. Preheat the oven to 350°F/180°C. Bake the pastry shells in the oven for 15–20 minutes. Let cool.

• Place the blueberries, crème de cassis, and confectioners' sugar in a pan and warm through so that the berries become shiny but do not burst. Let cool.

• To make the filling, melt the chocolate in a heatproof bowl set over a pan of simmering water, then let cool slightly. Whip the cream until stiff and fold in the sour cream and chocolate.

• Remove the pastry shells to a serving plate and divide the chocolate filling between them, smoothing the surface with a spatula, then top with the blueberries.

MAKES 8
PIE DOUGH
scant 1 cup all-purpose flour
4 oz/115 g butter, cut into small
    pieces
1 tbsp confectioners' sugar, sifted
1 small egg yolk
2–3 tsp cold water

FILLING
3 egg yolks
1/3 cup superfine sugar
3 tbsp all-purpose flour
1 cup milk

TOPPING
3 oz/85 g chocolate
1 tbsp honey
1/4 cup heavy cream
generous 1/3 cup toasted hazelnuts,
    chopped

Hazelnut Cream Pies

These elegant little pies look particularly attractive with their sprinkling of chopped toasted hazelnuts. They make a terrific dessert as well as a delicious teatime or coffee-time treat.

• To make the pie dough, sift the flour into a bowl and rub in the butter and sugar until the mixture resembles bread crumbs. Add the egg, and a little cold water to form a dough. Wrap the dough and let chill in the refrigerator for 30 minutes.

• Roll out the pie dough and use it to line an 8-cup muffin pan. Let chill in the refrigerator for about 20 minutes. Preheat the oven to 375°F/190°C. Bake the pies for 12–15 minutes. Let cool in the muffin pan.

• To make the filling, beat the egg yolks and superfine sugar in a heatproof bowl until pale and thick, add the flour, a little at a time, and mix to combine. Bring the milk to a boil and pour it over the egg mixture, whisking all the time, and beat well. Pour back into a clean pan and bring to a boil over low heat, stirring constantly. Boil for 1 minute, then pour into a cold bowl and stir. Let cool, stirring occasionally.

• To make the topping, melt the chocolate with the honey in a heatproof bowl set over a pan of barely simmering water. When melted, remove from the heat and stir in the cream. Let cool.

• Spoon the filling into each pie, cover with the melted chocolate mixture, and sprinkle with the nuts. Transfer to a serving dish and serve.

SERVES 4

2 ripe pears

4 tbsp butter

1 cup fresh white bread crumbs

generous 1/3 cup shelled pecans,
  chopped

generous 1/8 cup muscovado sugar

finely grated rind of 1 orange

3 1/2 oz/100 g phyllo pastry, thawed
  if frozen

6 tbsp orange blossom honey

2 tbsp orange juice

sifted confectioners' sugar,
  for dusting

strained plain yogurt, to serve
  (optional)

Pear and Pecan Strudel

Phyllo pastry is wrapped round a nutty pear filling in this easy-to-make strudel. It is delicious served warm. When working with phyllo pastry, it is important to keep it covered until you are ready to use it, otherwise the pastry will dry out very quickly.

• Preheat the oven to 400°F/200°C. Peel, core, and chop the pears. Melt 1 tablespoon of the butter in a skillet and gently sauté the bread crumbs until golden. Transfer the bread crumbs to a bowl and add the pears, nuts, muscovado sugar, and orange rind. Place the remaining butter in a small pan and heat until melted.

• Set aside 1 sheet of phyllo pastry, keeping it well wrapped, and brush the remaining phyllo sheets with a little melted butter. Spoon the nut filling onto the first phyllo sheet, leaving a 1-inch/2.5-cm margin around the edge. Build up the strudel by placing buttered phyllo sheets on top of the first, spreading each one with nut filling as you build up the layers. Drizzle the honey and orange juice over the top.

• Fold the short ends over the filling, then roll up, starting at a long side. Carefully lift onto a baking sheet, with the join uppermost. Brush with any remaining melted butter and crumple the reserved sheet of phyllo pastry around the strudel. Bake for 25 minutes, or until golden and crisp. Dust with sifted confectioners' sugar and serve warm with strained plain yogurt, if using.

MAKES 6
PIE DOUGH
scant 1¼ cups all-purpose flour
pinch of salt
4 tbsp butter, cut into small pieces
4 tbsp lard or vegetable shortening,
    cut into small pieces
2–3 tbsp cold water

FILLING
4 tbsp cornstarch
1¾ cups canned coconut milk
grated rind and juice of 2 limes
2 eggs, separated
scant 1 cup superfine sugar

Lime and Coconut Meringue Pies

There is a hint of Caribbean flavor to this delightful variation on the classic lemon meringue pie. They are delicious served hot or cold. Add a teaspoon of coconut liqueur, such as Malibu, or white rum to the filling with the lime juice and sugar, if you like.

• To make the pie dough, sift the flour and salt into a large bowl and rub in the butter and fat with the fingertips until the mixture resembles bread crumbs. Add the water and work the mixture together until a soft dough has formed. Wrap the dough and let chill in the refrigerator for 30 minutes.

• Preheat the oven to 350°F/180°C. Roll out the pie dough and use to line 6 tart pans, 4 inches/10 cm in diameter (1¼ inches/3 cm deep). Line with parchment paper and dried beans. Bake in the oven for 15 minutes. Remove from the oven and take out the paper and beans. Reduce the oven temperature to 325°F/160°C.

• To make the filling, place the cornstarch in a pan with a little of the coconut milk and stir to make a smooth paste. Stir in the rest of the coconut milk. Gradually bring to a boil over low heat, stirring constantly. Cook, stirring, for 3 minutes until thickened. Remove from the heat and add the lime rind and juice, egg yolks, and 4 tablespoons of the sugar. Pour the mixture into the pastry shells.

• Place the egg whites in a clean, greasefree bowl and whisk until very stiff, then gradually whisk in the remaining sugar, keeping a firm consistency. Pipe the meringue into peaks over the filling to cover it completely or cover the filling with the meringue and swirl gently with a spatula. Bake the pies in the oven for 20 minutes, or until the tops are lightly browned. Serve hot or cold.

For many people a meal is simply not complete without a homemade dessert. If you are one of those for whom neither a bowl of fresh fruit nor a tray of cheese and crackers will do, then this really is the chapter for you. It is packed with recipes for the most mouthwatering pies imaginable—some tried and trusted favorites, some imaginative variations on a familiar theme, and others that offer new and exciting combinations of flavors.

Hardly surprisingly, fruit pies take a starring role, but you might be amazed at the range and variety, from fruits of the forest to fruits of the tropics. Even well-loved friends, such as apple pie, get more than one makeover, appearing in a variety of delicious and unexpected guises. Of course, there are classics too, and these remain untouched—who can improve on Tarte au Citron?

DESSERT TREATS

Chocoholics need not despair—there are lots of fabulous treats for them, from the ever-popular Chocolate Chiffon Pie to the unusual and imaginative Chocolate Crumble Pie with its nut-and-biscuit topping. Fans of meringue toppings—always popular with kids—will also discover some clever new ideas.

All these dessert pies are great for both entertaining and family meals, especially at weekends when everyone's home and there's that little extra time for preparation. That said, they're not all immensely time-consuming. In fact, it's more likely you'll need the extra time for a post-prandial snooze to sleep off an irresistible second helping.

SERVES 6

PIE DOUGH

scant 2 cups all-purpose flour

pinch of salt

scant 2/3 cup superfine sugar

4 oz/115 g butter, cut into
    small pieces

1 egg

1 egg yolk

few drops vanilla extract

2–3 tsp water

sifted confectioners' sugar,
    for sprinkling

FILLING

4 tbsp apricot preserve

2 oz/55 g amaretti or ratafia cookies,
    crumbled

1 lb 14 oz–2 lb 4 oz/850 g–1 kg pears,
    peeled and cored

1 tsp ground cinnamon

1/2 cup raisins

1/3 cup packed brown or raw sugar

Pear Pie

Pears are a very popular fruit in Italy. In this recipe they are flavored with almonds, cinnamon, raisins, and apricot preserve. Choose ripe pears that are still firm. Don't peel and slice them in advance or the flesh will discolor and spoil the appearance of the dessert.

• To make the dough, sift the flour and salt onto a counter, make a well in the center, and add the sugar, butter, egg, egg yolk, vanilla extract, and most of the water.

• Using the fingers, gradually work the flour into the other ingredients to form a smooth dough, adding more water if necessary. Wrap the dough and let chill in the refrigerator for at least 1 hour.

• Preheat the oven to 400°F/200°C. Roll out three-quarters of the dough and use to line a shallow 10-inch/25-cm cake pan or deep tart pan. To make the filling, spread the preserve over the base and sprinkle with the crushed cookies.

• Slice the pears very thinly. Arrange over the cookies in the pastry shell. Sprinkle with cinnamon, then with raisins, and finally with brown sugar.

• Roll out a thin sausage shape using one-third of the remaining pie dough, and place around the edge of the pie. Roll the remainder into thin sausages and arrange in a lattice over the pie, 4 or 5 strips in each direction, attaching them to the strip around the edge.

• Cook in the preheated oven for 50 minutes until golden brown and cooked through. Let cool, then serve the pie warm or chilled, sprinkled with sifted confectioners' sugar.

SERVES 4

PIE DOUGH

2 cups all-purpose flour, plus extra
   for dusting

pinch of salt

¼ cup superfine sugar

9 oz/250 g butter, cut into small piece

1 egg

1 egg yolk

1 tbsp water

FILLING

3 tbsp black currant or plum preserve

generous ⅜ cup chopped toasted
   mixed nuts

2 lb 2 oz/950 g cooking apples

1 tbsp lemon juice

1 tsp apple pie spice

⅜ cup golden raisins

1¾ oz/50 g grapes, halved and
   seeded

generous ⅓ cup packed brown sugar

confectioners' sugar, for dusting

ice cream, to serve

Apple Lattice Pie

Apple pie spice is a blend of ground aromatic spices used in baking. It usually contains nutmeg, cloves, and cinnamon, and may also contain other spices. Although the flavor is quite similar, it is not the same as allspice.

• To make the pie dough, sift the flour and salt into a bowl. Make a well in the center and add the superfine sugar, butter, egg, egg yolk, and water. Mix together to form a smooth dough, adding more water if necessary. Wrap the dough and let chill in the refrigerator for 1 hour.

• Preheat the oven to 400°F/200°C. Shape about three-quarters of the dough into a ball and roll out on a lightly floured counter into a circle large enough to line a shallow 10-inch/25-cm tart pan. Fit it into the pan and trim the edge. Roll out the remaining pie dough and cut into long strips about ½ inch/1 cm wide.

• To make the filling, spread the preserve evenly over the base of the pastry shell, then sprinkle over the toasted nuts. Peel and core the apples, then cut them into thin slices. Place them in a bowl with the lemon juice, apple pie spice, golden raisins, grapes, and brown sugar. Mix together gently. Spoon the mixture into the pastry shell, spreading it out evenly.

• Arrange the pie dough strips in a lattice over the top of the pie. Moisten with a little water, seal, and trim the edges. Bake for 50 minutes until golden. Dust with confectioners' sugar. Serve at once with ice cream.

SERVES 8

PIE DOUGH

scant 1¼ cups all-purpose flour

1 tsp baking powder

4 oz/115 g unsalted butter, cut into
    small pieces

generous ¼ cup superfine sugar

1 egg yolk

1–2 tsp cold water

FILLING

⅔ cup heavy cream

⅔ cup milk

8 oz/225 g semisweet chocolate,
    chopped

2 eggs

CRUMBLE TOPPING

generous ½ cup packed brown sugar

¾ cup toasted pecans

4 oz/115 g semisweet chocolate

3 oz/85 g amaretti cookies

1 tsp unsweetened cocoa

Chocolate Crumble Pie

Amaretti are crunchy little Italian cookies, available from supermarkets and delicatessens. Although they have a strong almond flavor, they are actually made from apricot kernels.

• To make the pie dough, sift the flour and baking powder into a large bowl, rub in the butter, and stir in the sugar, then add the egg and a little water to bring the dough together. Turn the dough out, and knead briefly. Wrap the dough and let chill in the refrigerator for 30 minutes.

• Preheat the oven to 375°F/190°C. Roll out the pie dough and use to line a 9-inch/23-cm loose-bottom tart pan. Prick the pastry shell with a fork. Line with parchment paper and fill with dried beans. Bake in the oven for 15 minutes. Remove from the oven and take out the paper and beans. Reduce the oven temperature to 350°F/180°C.

• Bring the cream and milk to a boil in a pan, remove from the heat, and add the chocolate. Stir until melted and smooth. Beat the eggs and add to the chocolate mixture, mix thoroughly and pour into the shell. Bake for 15 minutes, remove from the oven, and let rest for 1 hour.

• When you are ready to serve the pie, place the topping ingredients in the food processor and pulse to chop. (If you do not have a processor, place the sugar in a large bowl, chop the nuts and chocolate with a large knife, and crush the cookies, then add to the bowl with the cocoa and mix well.) Sprinkle over the pie, then serve it in slices.

SERVES 8

PIE DOUGH

3 oz/85 g butter, cut into small pieces,
    plus extra for greasing

scant 1¼ cups all-purpose flour

1 tbsp water

1 egg, separated

sugar lumps, crushed, for sprinkling

FILLING

1 lb 5 oz/600 g prepared plums
    (damsons, rhubarb, or
    gooseberries)

⅓ cup packed brown sugar

1 tbsp ground ginger

One Roll Fruit Pie

This is an easy way to make a pie—once you have rolled out the pastry and filled it with fruit, you just turn the edges in. If the pastry breaks when you are shaping it into a circle, don't panic—just patch and seal, because the overall effect of this pie is quite rustic.

• Grease a large baking sheet with a little butter and set aside until required.

• To make the pie dough, place the flour and butter in a mixing bowl and rub in the butter with the fingertips until the mixture resembles bread crumbs. Add the water and work the mixture together until a soft dough has formed. Form into a ball. Wrap the dough and let chill in the refrigerator for 30 minutes.

• Preheat the oven to 400°F/200°C. Roll out the chilled dough to a circle about 14 inches/35 cm in diameter.

• Transfer the dough circle to the center of the prepared baking sheet. Lightly beat the egg yolk, then brush the dough with it.

• To make the filling, mix the plums with the brown sugar and ground ginger. Pile it into the center of the dough.

• Turn in the edges of the dough circle all the way around. Lightly beat the egg white, then brush the surface of the dough with it, and sprinkle with the crushed sugar lumps.

• Bake in the preheated oven for 35 minutes, or until golden brown. Serve warm.

SERVES 8

PIE DOUGH

scant 1¼ cups all-purpose flour, plus
 extra for dusting
½ tsp salt
¼ tsp superfine sugar
3½ tbsp butter, cut into small pieces
3 tbsp vegetable shortening, cut into
 small pieces
1–2½ tbsp cold water

FILLING

1 lb 2 oz/500 g orange-fleshed
 sweet potatoes
3 eggs, beaten
½ cup packed brown sugar
1½ cups canned evaporated milk
3 tbsp butter, melted

2 tsp vanilla extract
1 tsp ground cinnamon
1 tsp ground nutmeg or freshly
 grated nutmeg
½ tsp salt
whipped cream, to serve

Sweet Potato Pie

For a light, flaky pie dough, handle the dough as little as possible. If it is difficult to roll out, roll it between sheets of waxed paper. If the mixture isn't completely smooth after you have beaten in the eggs and sugar, press it through a fine strainer first.

• To make the pie dough, sift the flour, salt, and sugar into a bowl. Add the butter and vegetable shortening and rub in with the fingertips until the mixture resembles fine bread crumbs. Sprinkle over 2 tablespoons of the water and mix with a fork to make a soft dough. If the pie dough is too dry, sprinkle in an extra 1/2 tablespoon of water. Wrap the dough and let chill in the refrigerator for at least 1 hour.

• Meanwhile, bring a large pan of water to a boil over high heat. Peel and add the sweet potatoes and cook for 15 minutes. Drain, then cool them under cold running water. When cool, cut each into 8 wedges. Put the sweet potatoes in a separate bowl and beat in the eggs and brown sugar until very smooth. Beat in the remaining ingredients, then set aside until required.

• When ready to bake, preheat the oven to 425°F/220°C. Roll out the pie dough on a lightly floured counter into a thin 11-inch/28-cm circle and use to line a deep 9-inch/23-cm pie plate or pie pan (about 1¼ inches/4 cm deep). Trim off the excess pie dough and press the floured fork around the edge.

• Prick the base of the pastry shell all over with the fork. Line with parchment paper and fill with dried beans. Bake in the oven for 12 minutes until lightly golden.

• Remove the pastry shell from the oven and take out the paper and beans. Pour the filling into the pastry shell, and return to the oven for an additional 10 minutes. Reduce the oven temperature to 325°F/160°C and bake for an additional 35 minutes. Let cool on a wire rack. Serve warm or at room temperature with whipped cream.

SERVES 4

PIE DOUGH

generous 1⅜ cups all-purpose flour,
plus extra for dusting

3½ oz/100 g butter, cut into small
pieces, plus extra for greasing

generous ⅜ cup confectioners'
sugar, sifted

finely grated rind of 1 orange

1 egg yolk, beaten

3 tbsp milk

FILLING

7 oz/200 g semisweet chocolate,
broken into small pieces

2 eggs, separated

generous ⅓ cup milk

½ cup superfine sugar

8 amaretti cookies, crushed

ORANGE CREAM

1 tbsp orange-flavored liqueur,
such as Cointreau

1 tbsp finely grated orange rind,
plus extra to decorate

½ cup heavy cream

Chocolate Orange Pie

Chocolate and orange are flavors that were made for each other. If time is limited, just serve with plain whipped cream. If you're serving this to children, you could substitute orange juice for the orange liqueur.

• To make the pie dough, sift the flour into a bowl. Rub in the butter with the fingertips until the mixture resembles bread crumbs. Mix in the confectioners' sugar, orange rind, egg yolk, and milk. Turn out onto a lightly floured counter and knead briefly. Wrap the dough and let chill in the refrigerator for 30 minutes.

• Preheat the oven to 350°F/180°C. Grease a 9-inch/23-cm tart pan with butter. Roll out two-thirds of the pie dough to a thickness of ¼ inch/5 mm and use to line the base and side of the tart pan.

• To make the filling, melt the chocolate in a heatproof bowl set over a pan of barely simmering water. Beat in the egg yolks, then the milk. Remove from the heat. In a separate, greasefree bowl, whisk the egg whites until stiff, then stir in the superfine sugar. Fold the egg whites into the chocolate mixture, then stir in the cookies. Spoon into the pastry shell.

• Roll out the remaining pie dough, cut into strips, and use to form a lattice over the pie. Bake in the preheated oven for 1 hour.

• To make the orange cream, beat the liqueur, orange rind, and cream together. Remove the pie from the oven, decorate with orange rind, and serve with the orange cream.

SERVES 4

FILLING

1⅝ cups blueberries

1⅝ cups raspberries

1⅝ cups blackberries

½ cup superfine sugar

2 tbsp confectioners' sugar, to decorate

whipped cream, to serve

PIE DOUGH

scant 1⅜ cups all-purpose flour, plus extra for dusting

generous ¼ cup ground hazelnuts

3½ oz/100 g butter, cut into small pieces, plus extra for greasing

finely grated rind of 1 lemon

1 egg yolk, beaten

4 tbsp milk

Forest Fruit Pie

This pie is absolutely brimming with fruit. You can substitute any colorful berries, such as loganberries or bilberries. Ground hazelnuts and lemon rind are added to the pie dough for extra flavor, but you could use ground pistachios and lime rind if you like.

• Place the fruit in a pan with 3 tablespoons of the superfine sugar and let simmer gently, stirring frequently, for 5 minutes. Remove the pan from the heat.

• Sift the flour into a bowl, then add the hazelnuts. Rub in the butter with the fingertips until the mixture resembles bread crumbs, then sift in the remaining sugar. Add the lemon rind, egg yolk, and 3 tablespoons of the milk and mix. Turn out onto a lightly floured counter and knead briefly. Wrap and let chill in the refrigerator for 30 minutes.

• Preheat the oven to 375°F/190°C. Grease an 8-inch/20-cm pie dish with butter. Roll out two-thirds of the pie dough to a thickness of 5 mm/¼ inch and use it to line the base and side of the dish. Spoon the fruit into the pastry shell. Brush the rim with water, then roll out the remaining pie dough to cover the pie. Trim and crimp round the edge, then make 2 small slits in the top and decorate with 2 leaf shapes cut out from the dough trimmings. Brush all over with the remaining milk. Bake for 40 minutes. Remove from the oven, sprinkle with the confectioners' sugar and serve with whipped cream.

SERVES 6–8

PIE DOUGH

scant 1¼ cups all-purpose flour,
   plus extra for dusting

2 tbsp superfine sugar

4 oz/115 g butter, cut into small
   pieces

1 tbsp water

FILLING

scant 2 cups milk

4½ oz/125 g creamed coconut

3 egg yolks

½ cup superfine sugar

generous ½ cup all-purpose flour,
   sifted

¼ cup grated coconut

¼ cup chopped candied pineapple

2 tbsp dark rum or pineapple juice

generous 1¼ cups whipped cream

chopped fresh fruit, to decorate
   (optional)

Coconut Cream Pie

For an extra treat, decorate this rich, creamy pie with some fresh tropical fruit, such as mango, pineapple, passion fruit, or carambola, and grated coconut, toasted.

• To make the pie dough, place the flour and sugar in a bowl and rub in the butter with the fingertips until the mixture resembles bread crumbs. Add the water and work the mixture together until a soft dough has formed. Wrap the dough and let chill in the refrigerator for 30 minutes.

• On a lightly floured counter, roll out the dough and use to line a 9½-inch/24-cm loose-bottom tart pan. Prick the base all over with a fork.

• Preheat the oven to 375°F/190°C. Line the pastry shell with parchment paper and fill with dried beans. Bake in the oven for 15 minutes. Remove from the oven and take out the paper and beans. Bake the pastry shell for an additional 15 minutes. Let cool.

• To make the filling, bring the milk and creamed coconut to just below boiling point in a pan over low heat, stirring to melt the coconut.

• In a bowl, whisk the egg yolks with the sugar until pale and fluffy. Whisk in the flour. Pour the hot milk over the egg mixture, stirring constantly. Return the mixture to the pan and heat gently, stirring constantly, for 8 minutes, or until thick. Let cool.

• Stir the grated coconut, candied pineapple, and rum into the coconut filling. Spread the filling evenly in the pastry shell. Spread over with whipped cream. Top with fruit, if using, and chill in the refrigerator until ready to serve.

SERVES 6

PIE DOUGH

scant 1⅝ cups all-purpose flour,
    plus extra for dusting

pinch of salt

5 oz/140 g butter

generous ¼ cup superfine sugar

2 egg yolks

1–2 tsp cold water

FILLING

5 oz/140 g semisweet chocolate

2 tbsp butter

scant 1¼ cups superfine sugar

2 tsp cornstarch

4 egg yolks

scant 1 cup ground hazelnuts

3 egg whites

Chocolate and Nut Meringue Pie

This gloriously rich and self-indulgent dessert is best served warm, rather than hot. Make sure that the meringue is spread evenly all over the chocolate filling to cover it completely, otherwise it will ooze out.

• To make the pie dough, sift the flour with the salt into a bowl. Cream the butter and sugar together in a separate bowl until pale and fluffy. Sift over the flour, in 2 batches, and mix in, alternating with the egg yolks. Add a little cold water, if necessary, to make a dough. Wrap the dough and let chill in the refrigerator for 30 minutes.

• Roll out the pie dough on a lightly floured counter and use to line a 9-inch/23-cm tart pan. Preheat the oven to 375°F/190°C.

• Prick the base of the tart shell with a fork. Line with parchment paper and fill with dried beans. Bake in the oven for 10 minutes. Remove from the oven and take out the paper and beans.

• To make the filling, break the chocolate into pieces and melt in a heatproof bowl set over a pan of barely simmering water. Remove from the heat and let cool slightly.

• Cream the butter with 6 tablespoons of the sugar until pale and fluffy. Beat in the cornstarch and egg yolks, one at a time. Fold in the melted chocolate and the ground nuts.

• Spoon in the chocolate filling into the cooled pastry shell. Return to the oven and bake for an additional 10 minutes.

• Whisk the egg whites in a clean, greasefree bowl until soft peaks form. Gradually whisk in the remaining sugar and continue to whisk until stiff and glossy. Spoon the meringue over the filling in the pastry shell, covering it completely. Return to the oven and bake for an additional 15 minutes until the meringue is lightly set and golden.

SERVES 8
8-inch/20-cm ready-made pastry shell

FILLING
2 small ripe bananas
1 mango, peeled, seeded, and sliced
3½ tbsp cornstarch
6 tbsp raw sugar
1¼ cups soy milk
⅔ cup coconut milk
1 tsp vanilla extract
toasted coconut chips, to decorate

Banana and Mango Pie

Bananas and mangoes are a great combination of colors and flavors, especially when topped with toasted coconut chips. Coconut chips are available in some supermarkets and most health-food stores. They are worth using as they look more attractive than dry shredded coconut.

• Peel and slice the bananas, then arrange half of them in the base of the pastry shell with half of the mango slices.
• Place the cornstarch and sugar in a pan and mix together. Whisk in the soy milk and coconut milk gradually until combined. Let simmer over low heat, whisking constantly, for 2–3 minutes until the mixture thickens.
• Stir in the vanilla extract, then spoon the mixture over the fruit. Top with the remaining fruit and the toasted coconut chips. Let chill in the refrigerator for at least 1 hour before serving.

SERVES 6

PIE DOUGH

4 oz/115 g semisweet chocolate,
    in pieces

scant 1⅝ cups all-purpose flour,
    plus extra for dusting

4 oz/115 g unsalted butter, cut
    into small pieces

4 tbsp ground almonds

few drops almond extract

1–2 tbsp cold water

FILLING

1½ cup blanched almonds

generous ½ cup superfine sugar

5 oz/140 g unsalted butter

2 egg yolks

4 egg whites

few drops almond extract

5–6 ripe peaches (or apricots)

GLAZE

4 tbsp peach (or apricot) preserve

1 tbsp peach (or apricot) brandy

Peach and Almond Pie

This is a very elegant and luxurious dessert that would make a grand finale to a dinner party or celebration meal. However, although it looks impressive, it's actually quite simple to make.

• To make the pie dough, melt the chocolate in a heatproof bowl set over a pan of barely simmering water. Remove from the heat and let cool slightly. Sift the flour into a bowl and rub in the butter with the fingertips until the mixture resembles bread crumbs. Make a well in the center and add the melted chocolate, ground almonds, almond extract, and enough water to mix to a dough. Knead lightly. Wrap the dough and let chill in the refrigerator for 30 minutes.

• Roll out the dough on a lightly floured counter. Use to line a 9-inch/23-cm loose-bottom tart pan. Let chill until ready to use.

• Preheat the oven to 375°F/190°C and place a baking sheet in it. Process the blanched almonds and sugar in a food processor, pulsing until finely ground. Do not overprocess. Add the butter and process until smooth. Add the egg yolk, egg whites, and almond extract and process briefly until combined.

• Peel, halve, and pit the peaches. Thinly slice the peach halves crosswise, keeping the slices together so that the halves remain in shape.

• Spoon the almond mixture into the tart shell and level out. Using a spatula, transfer the sliced peach halves to the pastry shell, then spread them out slightly like the spokes of a wheel.

• Place on the heated baking sheet and bake for 50 minutes, or until set and golden brown. Remove from the oven and let cool slightly on a wire rack.

• Meanwhile, heat the preserve and brandy in a small pan, stirring until melted. Brush the glaze over the top of the pie and serve warm.

SERVES 6–8

PIE DOUGH

scant 1¼ cups all-purpose flour,
    plus extra for dusting
½ tsp salt
4 oz/115 g cold unsalted butter,
    cut into small pieces
1 egg yolk, beaten with 2 tbsp
    cold water

FILLING

grated rind of 2–3 large lemons
⅔ cup lemon juice
½ cup superfine sugar
½ cup heavy cream or sour cream
3 eggs
3 egg yolks
confectioners' sugar, for dusting

Tarte au Citron

Few desserts can be more appealing to round off a meal on a hot evening than this creamy, tangy pie. Although it's a pretty color, it doesn't look especially exciting, but it is a taste sensation. It could be described as a classic French understatement.

• To make the pie dough, sift the flour and salt into a bowl. Using your fingertips, rub the butter into the flour until the mixture resembles fine bread crumbs. Add the egg yolk and water and stir to form a dough. Gather the dough into a ball. Wrap and let chill in a refrigerator for at least 1 hour.

• Preheat the oven to 400°F/200°C. Roll out the dough on a lightly floured counter and use to line a 9–10-inch/23–25-cm fluted, loose-based tart pan. Prick the base all over with a fork and line with a sheet of parchment paper and fill with dried beans.

• Bake in the preheated oven for 15 minutes. Remove from the oven and take out the paper and beans. Reduce the oven temperature to 375°F/190°C.

• To make the filling, beat the lemon rind, lemon juice, and sugar together until blended. Slowly beat in the cream, then beat in the eggs and yolks.

• Set the pastry shell on a baking sheet and pour in the filling. Transfer to the preheated oven and bake for 20 minutes until the filling is set.

• Let cool completely on a wire rack. Dust with confectioners' sugar before serving.

SERVES 8

NUT BASE

scant 2 cups shelled Brazil nuts

4 tbsp granulated sugar

4 tsp melted butter

FILLING

1 cup milk

2 tsp powdered gelatin

generous ½ cup superfine sugar

2 eggs, separated

8 oz/225 g semisweet chocolate,
    roughly chopped

1 tsp vanilla extract

⅔ cup heavy cream

2 tbsp chopped Brazil nuts,
    to decorate

Chocolate Chiffon Pie

If you prefer to use leaf gelatin, use about 1½ leaves and soften them in cold water for 5 minutes, then squeeze before dissolving in hot liquid. Vegetarians can substitute Gelozone, but agar-agar is not suitable because chocolate will prevent it from setting properly.

• Preheat the oven to 400°F/200°C. Place the whole Brazil nuts in a food processor and process until finely ground. Add the granulated sugar and melted butter and process briefly to combine. Tip the mixture into a 9-inch/23-cm round tart pan and press it onto the base and side with a spoon or your fingertips. Bake in the preheated oven for 8–10 minutes, or until light golden brown. Set aside to cool.

• Pour the milk into a heatproof bowl and sprinkle the gelatin over the surface. Let it soften for 2 minutes, then set over a pan of gently simmering water. Stir in half of the superfine sugar, both the egg yolks, and all the chocolate. Stir constantly over low heat for 4–5 minutes until the gelatin has dissolved and the chocolate has melted. Remove from the heat and beat until the mixture is smooth. Stir in the vanilla extract, wrap and let chill in the refrigerator for 45–60 minutes until starting to set.

• Whip the cream until it is stiff, then fold all but about 3 tablespoons into the chocolate mixture. Whisk the egg whites in a separate, clean, greasefree bowl until soft peaks form. Add 2 teaspoons of the remaining sugar and whisk until stiff peaks form. Fold in the remaining sugar, then fold the egg whites into the chocolate mixture. Pour the filling into the pastry shell and let chill in the refrigerator for 3 hours. Decorate the pie with the remaining whipped cream and the chopped nuts before serving.

SERVES 4

PIE DOUGH

generous 1 cup all-purpose flour,
    plus extra for dusting
3 oz/85 g butter, cut into small
    pieces, plus extra for greasing
¼ cup confectioners' sugar, sifted
finely grated rind of ½ lemon
½ egg yolk, beaten
1½ tbsp milk

FILLING

3 cooking apples
2 tbsp lemon juice
finely grated rind of 1 lemon
⅔ cup honey
3 cups fresh white or whole
    wheat bread crumbs
1 tsp allspice
pinch of ground nutmeg
whipped cream, to serve

Spiced Apple Pie

Apples and spice are a classic, ever-popular combination. This pie makes a fabulous dessert, whatever the occasion. Blended honey is fine for cooking, although it does tend to taste rather bland. Single blossom honeys are more expensive, but for a complementary flavor, you could use lemon blossom honey, and for a distinctive, flowery taste, try lavender honey.

• To make the pie dough, sift the flour into a bowl. Rub in the butter with the fingertips until the mixture resembles bread crumbs, then mix in the confectioners' sugar, lemon rind, egg yolk, and milk. Knead briefly. Wrap the dough and let chill in the refrigerator for 30 minutes.

• Preheat the oven to 400°F/200°C. Grease an 8-inch/20-cm tart pan with butter. Roll out the pie dough on a lightly floured counter to a thickness of ¼ inch/5 mm and use to line the base and side of the pan.

• To make the filling, core 2 of the apples and grate them into a bowl. Add half of the lemon juice and all the lemon rind, along with the honey, bread crumbs, and allspice. Mix together well. Spoon evenly into the pastry shell. Core and slice the remaining apple, and use to decorate the top of the pie. Brush the apple slices with the remaining lemon juice, then sprinkle over the nutmeg. Bake in the oven for 35 minutes, or until firm. Remove from the oven and serve at once with whipped cream.

SERVES 8

4½ oz/125 g butter, preferably
   unsalted, softened
generous ¾ cup superfine sugar

2 eggs, beaten
generous 1¼ cups ground almonds
3 oz/85 g milk chocolate, grated
9 oz/250 g ready-made puff pastry

Chocolate Almond Pithiviers

Pithiviers is a traditional French pastry filled with almond paste, named after a town in the Orléans region of France. It is customary to serve it on Twelfth Night. This version includes chocolate for an extra touch of luxury.

• Cream the butter and scant ⅔ cup of the sugar together until light and pale, then gradually add 1 egg, beating well between each addition. Fold in the almonds and the chocolate.

• Roll out the puff pastry and cut out 2 x 10-inch/25-cm diameter circles. Place 1 circle on a baking sheet and mound the almond mixture on top, leaving a 1¼-inch/3-cm edge. Brush the edge with the remaining egg. Place the second circle on top, seal the edge, and score the top with a swirling pattern. Let chill for 30 minutes.

• Preheat the oven to 400°F/200°C. Bake the Pithiviers for 15 minutes, then reduce the oven temperature to 375°F/190°C and bake for an additional 10 minutes.

• Remove the Pithiviers from the oven and sprinkle with the remaining sugar. Place under a preheated broiler and caramelize the sugar—if your oven is really hot, this should take less than 1 minute. Slice and serve warm.

SERVES 6

PIE BASE

butter, for greasing

2 egg whites

1 cup ground almonds

4 tbsp ground rice

scant ⅔ cup superfine sugar

¼ tsp almond extract

FILLING

8 oz/225 g semisweet chocolate, broken into small pieces

4 egg yolks

4 tbsp confectioners' sugar

4 tbsp whiskey

4 tbsp heavy cream

TO DECORATE

⅔ cup whipped cream

2 oz/55 g semisweet chocolate, grated

Crispy Chocolate Pie

The rich, whiskey-flavored chocolate filling makes this delicious almond-crust pie very tempting. If you don't like the pronounced flavor of whiskey, substitute brandy or cherry brandy—both of which go well with chocolate.

• Preheat the oven to 325°F/160°C. Grease an 8-inch/20-cm springform pan and line the base with parchment paper. Whisk the egg whites until stiff peaks form. Gently fold in the ground almonds, ground rice, superfine sugar, and almond extract. Spread the mixture over the base and side of the prepared pan. Bake in the preheated oven for 15 minutes.

• Meanwhile, to make the filling, place the chocolate in a heatproof bowl set over a pan of barely simmering water until melted. Remove from the heat and let cool slightly, then beat in the egg yolks, confectioners' sugar, whiskey, and heavy cream until thoroughly incorporated.

• Remove the tart pan from the oven and pour in the chocolate mixture. Cover with foil, return to the oven, and bake at the same temperature for 20–25 minutes, until set. Remove from the oven and let cool completely.

• Cut the pie into 6 slices. Decorate each slice with whipped cream and sprinkled grated chocolate. Serve at once.

SERVES 4–6

FILLING

6 peaches, peeled and sliced

4 tbsp superfine sugar

½ tbsp lemon juice

1½ tsp cornstarch

½ tsp almond or vanilla extract

vanilla or pecan ice cream, to serve

PIE TOPPING

scant 1¼ cups all-purpose flour

generous ½ cup superfine sugar

1½ tsp baking powder

½ tsp salt

3 oz/85 g butter, diced

1 egg

5–6 tbsp milk

Peach Cobbler

To peel the peaches for this unusual pie, cut a small cross in the stem end of each. Lower them into a pan of boiling water and leave for 10–30 seconds, depending on ripeness. Drain and cool under cold running water to prevent further cooking. Peel using a small knife.

• Preheat the oven to 425°F/220°C. Place the peaches in a 9-inch/23-cm square ovenproof dish that is also suitable for serving. Add the sugar, lemon juice, cornstarch, and almond extract and toss together. Bake the peaches in the oven for 20 minutes.

• Meanwhile, to make the topping, sift the flour, all but 2 tablespoons of the sugar, the baking powder, and salt into a bowl. Rub in the butter with the fingertips until the mixture resembles bread crumbs. Mix the egg and 5 tablespoons of the milk in a pitcher, then mix into the dry ingredients with a fork until a soft, sticky dough forms. If the dough seems too dry, stir in the extra tablespoon of milk.

• Reduce the oven temperature to 400°F/200°C. Remove the peaches from the oven and drop spoonfuls of the topping over the surface, without smoothing. Sprinkle with the remaining sugar, return to the oven, and bake for an additional 15 minutes, or until the topping is golden brown and firm—the topping will spread as it cooks. Serve hot or at room temperature with ice cream.

Special-occasion meals and celebrations need to end with a flourish, and serving one of these fabulous pies will demonstrate just how much you care. Some of them can be made wholly in advance, while others can be partially prepared, ready for the last-minute touches. This can be a real boon when you're organizing a special meal and/or entertaining guests, not just because it helps with scheduling your time, but also because it's reassuring to sit down to the appetizer knowing that a perfect dessert is waiting in all its glory in the refrigerator.

Custom dictates that certain foods should be served on particular occasions and this is all very well if you happen to like whatever the traditional dish is. However, if you don't, it can be quite difficult to think of a sufficiently special substitute. Well—

SPECIAL OCCASIONS

no longer. For example, lots of people are not keen on frosted fruit cake, so why go to all the trouble of making one? Celebrate a birthday with the fabulous-tasting and elegant-looking Blackberry Chocolate Flan instead. You could even place birthday candles in it if you like. Kids of all ages consider baked Alaska a magical treat and you can really push the boat out with the recipe for Baked Chocolate Alaska, with its double chocolate hit.

The converse is equally true. You don't have to wait for Thanksgiving to enjoy Sweet Pumpkin Pie with its warm spices. In fact, although these recipes are perfect for any celebration, they would be a special treat on any occasion, turning an ordinary meal into a feast and an everyday family supper into a party.

SERVES 8

PIE DOUGH

scant 1⅝ cups all-purpose flour

pinch of salt

4 oz/115 g butter, cut into small
  pieces

1 tbsp lard or vegetable shortening,
  cut into small pieces

generous ¼ cup golden superfine
  sugar

6 tbsp cold milk

FILLING

3 eggs

generous 1 cup muscovado sugar

1 tsp vanilla extract

pinch of salt

3 oz/85 g butter, melted

3 tbsp corn syrup

3 tbsp molasses

2 cups shelled pecans, roughly
  chopped

pecan halves, to decorate

whipped cream or vanilla ice cream,
  to serve

Pecan Pie

Pecan pie is a classic recipe from America's Deep South. Do try to obtain nuts as fresh as possible, as these have the sweetest and richest flavor. Served with a spoonful of whipped cream or ice cream, this pie is the perfect finale to a special meal.

• To make the pie dough, sift the flour and salt into a mixing bowl and rub in the butter and lard with the fingertips until the mixture resembles fine bread crumbs. Work in the superfine sugar and add the milk. Work the mixture into a soft dough. Wrap the dough and let chill in the refrigerator for 30 minutes.

• Preheat the oven to 400°F/200°C. Roll out the pie dough and use it to line a 9–10-inch/23–25-cm tart pan. Trim off the excess by running the rolling pin over the top of the tart pan. Line with parchment paper, and fill with dried beans. Bake in the oven for 20 minutes. Take out of the oven and remove the paper and dried beans. Reduce the oven temperature to 350°F/180°C. Place a baking sheet in the oven.

• To make the filling, place the eggs in a bowl and beat lightly. Beat in the muscovado sugar, vanilla extract, and salt. Stir in the butter, syrup, molasses, and chopped nuts. Pour into the pastry shell and decorate with the pecan halves.

• Place on the heated baking sheet and bake in the oven for 35–40 minutes until the filling is set. Serve warm or at room temperature with whipped cream or vanilla ice cream.

SERVES 4
butter, for greasing
2 eggs
generous ¾ cup superfine sugar,
    plus 4 tbsp

4 tbsp all-purpose flour
2 tbsp unsweetened cocoa
3 egg whites
4 cups good-quality chocolate
    ice cream

Baked Chocolate Alaska

This magical dessert is even more delicious and special when it is served with a black currant sauce. Cook a few black currants in a little orange juice over low heat until softened, blend to a purée and push through a nylon strainer to remove any seeds. Sweeten to taste by stirring in a little confectioners' sugar.

• Preheat the oven to 425°F/220°C. Grease a 7-inch/18-cm round cake pan and line the base with parchment paper.

• Whisk the eggs and the 4 tablespoons of sugar in a mixing bowl until very thick and pale. Sift the flour and cocoa together and carefully fold in.

• Pour into the prepared pan and bake in the preheated oven for 7 minutes, or until springy to the touch. Turn out and transfer to a wire rack to cool completely.

• Whisk the egg whites in a clean, greasefree bowl until soft peaks form. Gradually add the remaining sugar, whisking until you have a thick, glossy meringue. Place the sponge on a baking sheet. Soften the ice cream in the refrigerator and pile it onto the center to form a dome.

• Pipe or spread the meringue over the ice cream, making sure it is completely enclosed. (At this point the dessert can be frozen, if wished.)

• Return to the oven for 5 minutes, until the meringue is just golden. Serve at once.

SERVES 6

4 lb/1.8 kg sweet pumpkin

4 tbsp cold unsalted butter, in small
pieces, plus extra for greasing

1 cup all-purpose flour, plus extra
for dusting

¼ tsp baking powder

1½ tsp ground cinnamon

¾ tsp ground nutmeg

¾ tsp ground cloves

1 tsp salt

¼ cup superfine sugar

3 eggs

1¾ cups sweetened condensed milk

½ tsp vanilla extract

1 tbsp raw sugar

STREUSEL TOPPING

2 tbsp all-purpose flour

4 tbsp raw sugar

1 tsp ground cinnamon

2 tbsp cold unsalted butter,
in small pieces

generous ⅔ cup shelled
pecans, chopped

generous ⅔ cup shelled
walnuts, chopped

Sweet Pumpkin Pie

To roast pepitas, or pumpkin seeds, soak them in salt water overnight, then drain. Spread them out on a greased baking sheet. Sprinkle over a little salt for extra flavor. Bake in a preheated oven at 350°F/180°C for 20 minutes.

• Preheat the oven to 375°F/190°C. Halve the pumpkin, remove the seeds (pepitas), and set aside for roasting (see Cook's Tip). Remove and discard the stem and stringy insides. Place the pumpkin halves, face down, in a shallow baking pan and cover with foil. Bake in the preheated oven for 1½ hours, then remove from the oven and let cool. Scoop out the flesh and mash with a potato masher or purée it in a food processor. Drain away any excess liquid. Cover with plastic wrap and let chill until ready to use. It will keep for 3 days (or several months in a freezer).

• To make the pie dough, first grease a 9-inch/23-cm round pie dish with butter. Sift the flour and baking powder into a large bowl. Stir in ½ tsp cinnamon, ¼ tsp nutmeg, ¼ tsp cloves, ½ tsp salt, and all the superfine sugar. Rub in the butter with the fingertips until the mixture resembles fine bread crumbs, then make a well in the center. Lightly beat 1 egg and pour it into the well. Mix together with a wooden spoon, then use your hands to shape the dough into a ball. Place it on a clean counter lightly dusted with flour, and roll out to a circle large enough to line the pie dish. Use it to line the dish, then trim the edge. Cover dish with plastic wrap and let chill in the refrigerator for 30 minutes.

• Preheat the oven to 425°F/220°C. To make the filling, place the pumpkin purée in a large bowl, then stir in the condensed milk and remaining eggs. Add the remaining spices and salt, then stir in the vanilla extract and raw sugar. Pour into the pastry shell and bake for 15 minutes.

• Meanwhile, make the topping. Combine the flour, sugar, and cinnamon in a bowl, rub in the butter until crumbly, then stir in the nuts. Remove the pie from the oven and reduce the heat to 350°F/180°C. Sprinkle the topping over the pie, then bake for an additional 35 minutes. Remove from the oven and serve hot or cold.

SERVES 8

PIE DOUGH

1 cup all-purpose flour, plus
    extra for dusting

¼ tsp baking powder

½ tsp allspice

½ tsp salt

¼ cup sugar

6 tbsp cold unsalted butter, diced,
    plus extra for greasing

water, for sealing

1 beaten egg, plus extra for glazing

FILLING

2 lb/900 g pitted fresh or canned
    cherries, drained

½ tsp almond extract

2 tsp cherry brandy

¼ tsp allspice

¾ cup sugar

2 tbsp cornstarch

2 tbsp water

freshly whipped cream or
    ice cream, to serve

Latticed Cherry Pie

Cherry pie is traditionally served with a lattice top, but if you prefer, you can use the other circle of dough whole to cover the pie. Trim the edge, seal with water, crimp around the rim, then brush with beaten egg. Make two slits in the center with a sharp knife to let out the steam. Cut out small shapes, such as leaves, from any remaining dough and use to decorate.

• To make the pie dough, sift the flour and baking powder into a large bowl. Stir in ½ tsp allspice, ½ tsp salt, and ¼ cup sugar. Using the fingertips, rub in 4 tablespoons of butter until the mixture resembles fine bread crumbs, then make a well in the center. Pour the beaten egg into the well. Mix with a wooden spoon, then shape the mixture into a dough. Cut the dough in half and use your hands to roll each half into a ball. Wrap the dough and let chill in the refrigerator for 30 minutes.

• Preheat the oven to 425°F/220°C. Grease a 9-inch/23-cm round pie dish with butter. Roll out the dough into 2 circles, each 12 inches/30 cm in diameter. Use one to line the pie dish. Trim the edge, leaving an overhang of ½ inch/1 cm.

• To make the filling, place half the cherries and the remaining sugar in a large pan. Bring to a simmer over low heat, stirring, for 5 minutes, or until the sugar has melted. Stir in the almond extract, brandy, and remaining allspice. In a separate bowl, mix the cornstarch and water to form a paste. Remove the pan from the heat, stir in the cornstarch, then return to the heat and stir constantly until the mixture boils and thickens. Let cool a little. Stir in the remaining cherries, pour into the pastry shell, then dot with the remaining butter.

• Cut the dough circle into long strips ½ inch/1 cm wide. Lay 5 strips evenly across the top of the filling in the same direction, folding back every other strip. Now lay 6 strips crosswise over the strips, folding back every other strip each time you add another crosswise strip, to form a lattice. Trim off the ends and seal the edges with water. Use your fingers to crimp around the rim, then brush the top with beaten egg. Cover with foil, then bake for 30 minutes. Remove from the oven, discard the foil, then return the pie to the oven for an additional 15 minutes, or until cooked and golden. Serve warm with freshly whipped cream or ice cream.

SERVES 6

PIE DOUGH

1 cup all-purpose flour, plus extra
    for dusting

generous ¼ cup unsweetened cocoa

½ cup confectioners' sugar

pinch of salt

3 oz/85 g unsalted butter, cut into
    small pieces

½ egg yolk

FILLING

1¼ cups heavy cream

6 oz/175 g blackberry preserve

8 oz/225 g semisweet chocolate,
    broken into pieces

2 tbsp unsalted butter, cut into
    small pieces

SAUCE

1 lb 8 oz/675 g blackberries,
    plus extra for decoration

1 tbsp lemon juice

2 tbsp superfine sugar

2 tbsp crème de cassis

Blackberry Chocolate Flan

This richly flavored flan looks superb and tastes wonderful—a perfect choice for a special occasion. It would also work well with raspberries and raspberry preserve. If you can find crème de framboise, substitute it for the crème de cassis.

• To make the pie dough, sift the flour, cocoa, confectioners' sugar, and salt into a mixing bowl and make a well in the center. Place the butter and egg yolk in the well and gradually mix in the dry ingredients, using a pastry blender or two forks. Knead lightly and form into a ball. Wrap the dough and let chill in the refrigerator for 1 hour.

• Preheat the oven to 350°F/180°C. Roll out the dough on a lightly floured counter. Use it to line a 12 x 4-inch/ 30 x 10-cm rectangular tart pan and prick the pastry shell with a fork. Line the base with parchment paper and fill with dried beans. Bake in the preheated oven for 15 minutes. Remove the tart pan, paper and beans from the oven, and set aside to cool.

• To make the filling, place the cream and preserve in a pan and bring to a boil over low heat. Remove from the heat and stir in the chocolate and then the butter until melted and smooth. Pour the mixture into the pastry shell and set aside to cool.

• To make the sauce, put the blackberries, lemon juice, and superfine sugar in a food processor and process until smooth. Strain through a nylon sieve into a bowl and stir in the crème de cassis. Set aside.

• Remove the flan from the pan and place on a serving plate. Arrange the remaining blackberries on top and brush with a little blackberry and liqueur sauce. Serve the flan with the remaining sauce on the side.

SERVES 6

8 oz/225 g ready-prepared pie dough

FILLING

3 eggs

scant 2/3 cup superfine sugar

generous 3/8 cup all-purpose flour,
    plus extra for dusting

1 tbsp confectioners' sugar

pinch of salt

1 tsp vanilla extract

1¾ cups milk

2/3 cup plain yogurt

5½ oz/150 g semisweet chocolate,
    broken into pieces

2 tbsp Kirsch

TO DECORATE

2/3 cup sour cream

8 oz/225 g semisweet chocolate
    shavings or caraque

Boston Chocolate Pie

To make chocolate caraque, spread melted chocolate in a thin layer on a cold surface and let cool and set. Scrape off curls with a spatula held firmly at an angle.

• Preheat the oven to 400°F/200°C. Roll out the pie dough and use to line a 9-inch/23-cm loose-bottom tart pan. Prick the base with a fork, line with parchment paper, and fill with dried beans. Bake in the preheated oven for 20 minutes. Remove the beans and paper and return the pastry shell to the oven for an additional 5 minutes. Remove from the oven and place on a wire rack to cool.

• To make the filling, beat the eggs and superfine sugar in a heatproof bowl until fluffy. Sift in the flour, confectioners' sugar, and salt. Stir in the vanilla extract.

• Bring the milk and yogurt to a boil in a small pan and strain it over the egg mixture. Set the bowl over a pan of barely simmering water. Stir the custard until it coats the back of a spoon.

• Gently heat the chocolate with the Kirsch in a separate small pan until the chocolate has melted. Stir into the custard. Remove from the heat and stand the bowl in cold water. Let cool.

• Pour the chocolate mixture into the pastry shell. Spread the sour cream over the chocolate and decorate with chocolate shavings or caraque.

Index